MEGA BOOKS

SHARKS

NINA FILIPEK
AND SOPHIE GILES

Gareth Stevens
PUBLISHING

BE A Super Spotter

Study these pictures and look out for them as you read this book. Can you answer the super spotter questions?

Whose eye is this?

Which shark has a mouth like this?

Whose spotty disguise is this?

Whose tooth is this?

Please visit our website, www.garethstevens.com. For a free color catalog of all our high-quality books, call toll free 1-800-542-2595 or fax 1-877-542-2596.

Published in 2025 by
Gareth Stevens Publishing
2544 Clinton St.
Buffalo, NY 14224

Written and edited by: Christiane Gunzi and Chez Picthall
Designer: Paul Calver
Editorial assistant: Katy Rayner
Vehicle consultant: Gary Boyd-Hope

Images: Page 4: *Dwarf lantern shark* – Dr Gregory R. Mann; all other images: Shutterstock (front cover: *Great white shark* – Willyam Bradberry, *Background* – Dudarev Mikhail; page 1: *Great white shark* – Mogens Trolle; page 3: *Whale shark* – Krzysztof Odziomek, *Blacktip reef shark* – Eric Isselee, *Nurse shark* – frantisekhojdysz, *Great white shark with seal* – Sergey Uryadnikov, *Mermaid's purse* – B. Speckart, *Bull shark head shot* – Willyam Bradberry, *Great white shark* – Joe Belanger, *Scalloped hammerhead shark* – Matt9122, *Blue shark* – Dray van Beeck, *Whale shark* – Krzysztof Odziomek, *Angel shark* – Stephen Nash, *Gray reef shark* – Willyam Bradberry, *Megalodon* – Catmando, *Shark fin soup* – 54613, *Leopard shark skin* – Christophe Rouziou; pages 4–5: *Background* – Rich Carey, *Whale shark* – Krzysztof Odziomek, *Caribbean reef shark* – VisionDive, *Leopard shark* – Aleksandr Sadkov, *Blacktip reef shark head shot* – zebra0209; pages 6–7: *Blacktip reef shark* – Eric Isselee, *Dorsal fin* – Jamen Percy, *Great white shark* – Jim Agronick, *Tail shot* – Sergey Uryadnikov; pages 8–9: *Background* – littlesam, *Nurse shark* – frantisekhojdysz, *Great white shark* – Stefan Pircher, *Six gill shark* – Greg Amptman, *Nurse shark with coral* – Matt9122; pages 10–11: *Great white shark* – Mogens Trolle, *Whale shark feeding* – Dudarev Mikhail, *Great white shark with seal* – Sergey Uryadnikov, *Tiger shark* – Matt9122, *Sand tiger shark* – MP cz; pages 12–13: *Young white shark* – Petra Christen, *Great white shark* – kbrowne41, *Young dogfish* – Susana_Martins, *Mermaid's purse* – B. Speckart; pages 14–15: *Background* – Willyam Bradberry, *Bull shark* – Willyam Bradberry, *Bull shark head shot* – Willyam Bradberry, *Bull shark feeding* – Willyam Bradberry, *Bull shark and divers* – Ciurzynski; pages 16–17: *Great white shark* – Jim Agronick, *Great white shark head shot* – Elsa Hoffmann, *Tooth* – BW Folsom, *Great white shark white belly* – VisionDive, *Seals* – Erwin Niemand, *Dolphins* – TAGSTOCK1, *Turtles* – Rich Carey, *Other sharks* – Fiona Ayerst; pages 18–19: *Background* – Rich Carey, *Scalloped hammerhead shark* – Matt9122, *Stingray* – Kristina Vackova, *Hammerhead shark close-up* – Matt9122, *Great Hammerhead shark* – Shane Gross; pages 20–21: *Blue shark* – Dray van Beeck, *Shoal of tuna* – Rich Carey, *Blue shark and boat* – Joost van Uffelen, *Blue shark from below* – Brandelet, *Squid* – Narchuk, *Anchovy* – evantravels, *Lobster* – Ethan Daniels, *Shrimp* – Bennyartist; pages 22–23: *Whale shark* – Krzysztof Odziomek, *Diver* – fenkieandreas, *Whale shark front on* – Krzysztof Odziomek, *Whale shark with remora fish* – Soren Egeberg Photography, *Plankton* – Johnlips, *Jellyfish* – pan demin, *Krill* – Dmytro Pylypenko; pages 24–25: *Background* – Vilainecrevette, *Angel shark* – Stephen Nash, *Flounder* – Beth Swanson, *Angel shark skin* – Stephen Nash, *Leopard shark* – Christophe Rouziou; pages 26–27: *Background* – littlesam, *Coral* – Jolanta Wojcicka, *Reef shark* – frantisekhojdysz, *Group of blacktip reef sharks* – Dray van Beeck, *Gray reef shark* – Willyam Bradberry, *Pink coral* – Le Do, *Angel fish* – serg_dibrova; pages 28–29: *Background* – Rich Carey, *Megalodon* – Catmando, *Megalodon tooth* – Jake Kohlberg, *Great white shark tooth* – BW Folsom, *Megalodon silhouette* – Catmando, *Man silhouette* – Vector Goddess, *Megalodon feeding* – Catmando; pages 30–31: *Great white shark* – Mogens Trolle, *Whale shark* – Krzysztof Odziomek, *Scalloped hammerhead shark* – Matt9122, *Shark fishing* – Emmanuel R Lacoste, *Shark fin soup* – 54613, *Angel shark* – Stephen Nash, *Great white shark* – Joe Belanger, *Background* – littlesam)

Cataloging-in-Publication Data

Names: Filipek, Nina. | Giles, Sophie.
Title: Sharks / by Nina Filipek and Sophie Giles.
Description: Buffalo, NY : Gareth Stevens Publishing, 2025. | Series: Mega books
Identifiers: ISBN 9781482468083 (pbk.) | ISBN 9781482468090 (library bound) | ISBN 9781482468106 (ebook)
Subjects: LCSH: Sharks--Juvenile literature.
Classification: LCC QL638.9 F47 2025 | DDC 590--dc23

Printed in the United States of America

CPSIA compliance information: Batch #CSGS25: For further information contact Gareth Stevens at 1-800-542-2595.

CONTENTS

What Is a Shark? 4
Shark Parts 6
Shark Senses 8

Shark Diet 10
Shark Pups 12
Bull Shark 14

Great White Shark 16
Hammerhead Shark 18
Blue Shark 20

Whale Shark 22
Masters of Disguise 24
Reef Sharks 26

Prehistoric Shark 28
Save Our Sharks! 30
Glossary & Index

WHAT IS A SHARK?

Sharks are an amazing group of fish, found in all the oceans of the world. They have been around since before the dinosaurs. Today, there are over 400 types, or species, of shark, from the tiny dwarf lantern shark to the gigantic whale shark.

Can you spot the dwarf lantern shark?

Fishy!

Sharks are fish. They have a smooth, pointed body shape, which is good for swimming, and a tail and fins for steering their way through the water.

Sharks in the dark

Researchers have discovered three deep-sea shark species that are bioluminescent, or luminous, meaning they can give off light. The kitefin shark, the blackbelly lanternshark, and the southern lanternshark are all able to do this. But researchers still need to learn how and why.

Shark skin

A shark's skin is tough and feels like sandpaper. It is made up of denticles, or tiny, sharp scales that are made of the same material as human teeth.

Leopard shark

The leopard shark's skin is patterned like a leopard's fur.

Breathe in

Sharks have gills for breathing underwater. Gills are openings on either side of the body behind the head. As they swim along, sharks take in oxygen from the water that passes over their gills.

Blacktip reef shark

SHARK PARTS

Unlike many other fish, sharks don't have bony skeletons. Their skeletons are made up of a light, bendy material called cartilage similar to the material that makes up your ears and nose. This allows sharks to move with ease and speed.

Sharks swim in an S shape through the water.

Why do sharks have a dorsal fin?

Dorsal fins

The dorsal fin is the one that sticks out above the water when a shark is swimming near the surface. It helps with balance. Without it, the shark would roll over. Some sharks have two dorsal fins.

Pectoral fins

The two pectoral fins under the body are used for steering and to lift the shark in the water as it swims.

Great white shark

Tail fins

The tail fin moves from side to side as the shark swims, and is important for generating power and speed in the water.

Great white shark

Can you point to?

a dorsal fin

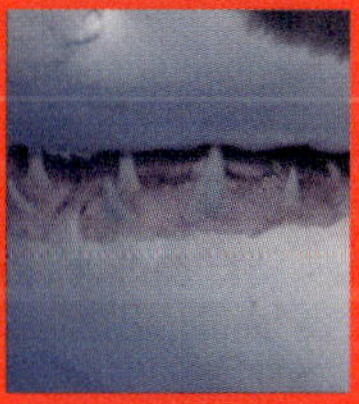

teeth

a tail

SHARK SENSES

All sharks have an excellent sense of smell and most have very good eyesight. They can smell their food, or prey, and detect movement in the water from a great distance away.

Most sharks' eyes are on either side of their head so they can see all around—except directly in front of their nose!

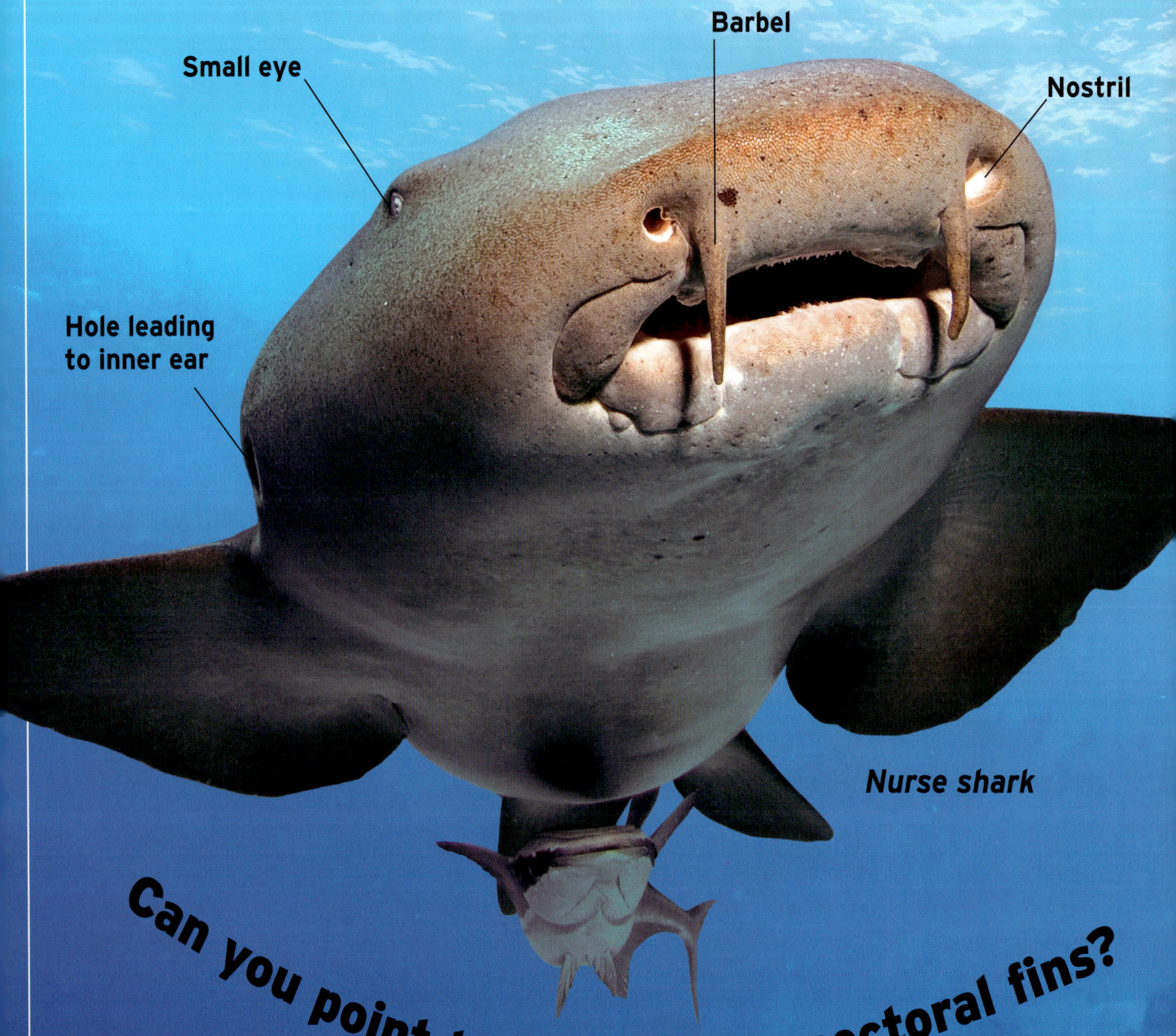

Nurse shark

Can you point to this shark's pectoral fins?

Nose-y!

A shark's nostrils are not used for breathing—just for smelling! The great white shark can smell the blood of an injured fish from 0.3 mile (0.5 km) away! It does this using sensors inside the nostril slits—also called nares—on either side of its nose.

Great white shark

Beady eyes

Sharks can see in the water much better than we can. Most sharks have eyelids that they can half close to protect their eyes if they are attacked, or when they are feeding.

Sixgill shark

Nurse shark

Barbels

Nostril barbels look like fleshy whiskers. They are used to feel and taste prey.

SHARK DIET

Sharks are fierce hunters of other fish in the sea. As well as eating fish, bigger sharks will eat sea turtles, seals, and penguins. However, some of the biggest sharks feed on the smallest of sea creatures, called plankton.

Great white shark

Filter feeder

The whale shark swims with its huge mouth wide open, scooping up plankton as it goes.

Surface attack

Great whites push their prey up to the surface as they attack. But this great white failed to catch a seal meal this time!

Great white shark

Huge appetite

The tiger shark has been called the "garbage can of the sea" because it will eat anything and everything. It has a massive appetite, and may swim more than 25 miles (40 km) a day in search of food.

Gas cans, car tires, and baseballs have all been found in the stomachs of tiger sharks!

Tiger shark

Terrible teeth

Sharks are famous for their sharp teeth. Sand tiger sharks have three rows of sharply pointed teeth, which curve backwards, to help them hold on to their prey.

Sand tiger shark

SHARK PUPS

Baby sharks are called pups. Most hatch from eggs inside the mother shark, then continue to grow and develop inside her until they are born. Mother sharks swim to safer waters, such as lagoons, to give birth, as the pups are left to look after themselves from the moment they are born.

What is a baby shark called?

White shark pup

The young shark is a miniature version of the adult.

Can you point to?

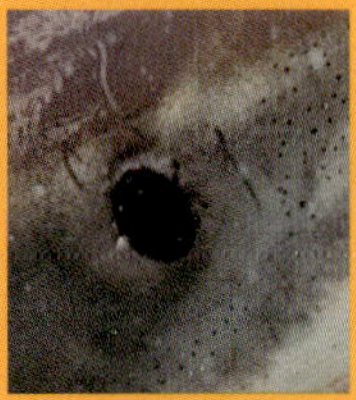

an eye

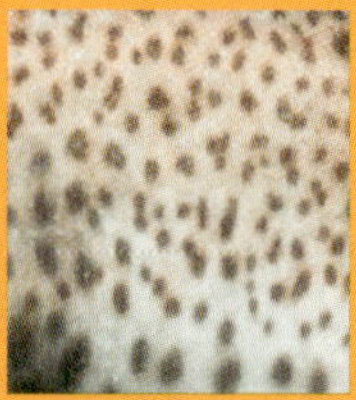

spotted skin

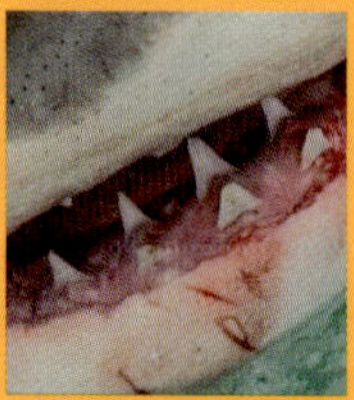

sharp teeth

Adult great white shark

Shark pups

Some types of shark have only a few pups, but many will have around 10. On average, only two out of a litter of 10 pups will survive and grow into adult sharks.

Tendrils attach to seaweed

Mermaid's purse

Mermaid's purse

While most sharks give birth to live pups, some sharks, such as dogfish, lay eggs. Inside this egg case (called a "mermaid's purse") there is a shark's egg. The shark grows inside and hatches after about six months.

Young dogfish

BULL SHARK

The bull shark is one of the most dangerous to humans as they often swim in warm waters by the shore. They can also live in fresh water, so they can swim up rivers too. They eat mainly fish but also turtles and other sharks, and some even attack hippos in rivers!

What does the bull shark eat?

Bull shark

Can you point to?

a diver

an eye

a dorsal fin

Poor eyesight

The bull shark usually hunts in murky waters where it can swim without being seen easily. It uses its good sense of smell to find its prey.

It has smaller eyes than most other sharks.

Bump and bite

Because these sharks can't see very well, they tend to bump into their prey first before they bite!

Bull shark feeding in the Pacific Ocean

Short and stocky

Bull sharks can grow up to 13 feet (4 m) long and weigh as much as 500 pounds (230 kg). However, it is wider and shorter than the great white.

The divers are keeping a safe distance from this bull shark.

GREAT WHITE SHARK

One of the world's largest and most famous sharks is the great white. You may have heard about these sharks attacking people, but this is rare. When sharks attack people, it is because they mistake them for their usual prey, such as whales, dolphins, seals, and other fish.

Why does it have sharp teeth?

Jaws!

Great whites can have up to 30,000 teeth in their lifetime. When they lose a tooth another one moves forward to take its place.

Actual size

White belly

The great white shark is actually gray and white. It has a white belly, but its body is gray on top so that it is not seen when swimming underneath prey.

Big tooth

This is the tooth of a great white. It grows up to 3 inches (7.5 cm) long. Even the sides of the tooth are sharp and jagged.

Great white shark's diet

seals

dolphins

turtles

other sharks

HAMMERHEAD SHARK

It is easy to see why this shark is called a hammerhead! Scientists think the unusual shape of its head helps the hammerhead to spot its prey. The eyes, set on each side of its head, give it a wide view of the sea all around.

What does this shark like to eat?

These sharks often swim in large groups, called schools.

Hide-and-seek

Why do you think this bluespotted ribbontail ray is hiding in the sand? Because the hammerhead shark likes to eat them!

Keeping cool

Hammerhead sharks are found in warm seas throughout the world. But in the hot summer months, they often swim to cooler waters.

Can you point to?

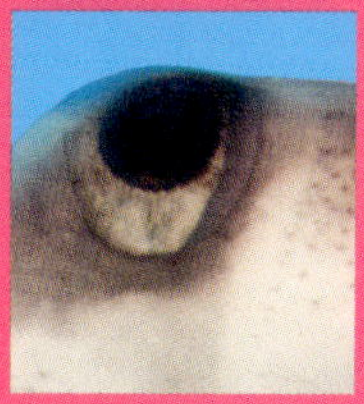

an eye

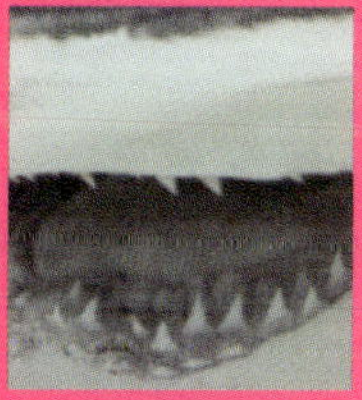

teeth

stingray

Great hammerhead

Most hammerhead sharks are small, but the largest, the great hammerhead shark, can grow up to 20 feet (6 m) long.

Great hammerhead shark

BLUE SHARK

This shark is one of the fastest swimmers in the sea. When chasing prey, it reaches speeds of up to 25 miles (40 km) per hour. Known as the "wolf of the sea," the blue shark travels many thousands of miles each year across the world's oceans.

Fast food

These sharks will eat smaller fish, such as tuna or anchovies, by swimming straight through the middle of the shoal with an open mouth. They eat as many as they can catch while on the move!

A shoal of small tuna

This blue shark is swimming underneath a boat!

Can you point to?

a squid

an eye

tuna fish

Midnight feast

The blue shark prefers cooler waters and is most often found in the deeper parts of the North Atlantic. For some of the year, it moves to shallower waters at night, where food is more plentiful, in order to feed.

Deeper waters are cooler

Blue shark's diet

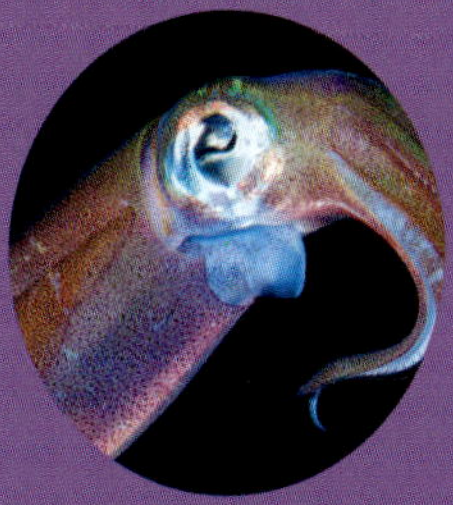

squid

anchovies

lobsters

shrimps

WHALE SHARK

The whale shark is the biggest shark in the world, and grows up to 40 feet (12 m) in length. It is harmless to humans as it only feeds on tiny animals and its 300 teeth are only about 0.1 inch (3 mm) long. Despite their huge size, whale sharks are generally friendly, and even let scuba divers swim close by.

Is this shark dangerous to people?

Open wide!

This shark swims with its enormous mouth wide open. As water flows in, it draws small creatures in with it. The water then passes out through its gills, and the food is swallowed.

Can you point to?

an eye

jellyfish

remora fish

In the fast lane

A shoal of remora fish is hitching a ride on the whale shark. Remoras can use a sucker on their head to attach themselves to the whale shark.

Whale shark's diet

plankton

jellyfish

krill

MASTERS OF DISGUISE

The angel shark has a flattened body and pectoral fins that extend from its body, which look a little like an angel's wings. It only grows to about 6.5 feet (2 m) long at most. Its teeth are tiny triangles, but they are as sharp as needles!

Angel shark

Color camouflage

The angel shark's skin color matches the sand on the sea bed, to fool its prey and to help it hide from other, fiercer sharks. This is called camouflage.

Flounder are the prey of the angel shark.

Hidden danger

The angel shark buries itself in the sand on the ocean bed. With only its eyes peeping out, it waits for passing prey, such as flounder or halibut. Then it darts quickly upwards, attacking from below.

Leopard shark

Though its body is not as flat as the angel shark, the leopard shark also uses camouflage to hide on the ocean floor as it hunts its prey.

Leopard shark

REEF SHARKS

Sharks that live in the shallow tropical waters around coral reefs are called reef sharks. These include the whitetip, blacktip, gray, and Caribbean reef sharks.

Can you point to?

coral

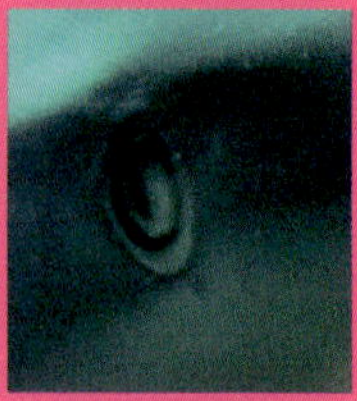

an eye

a tail

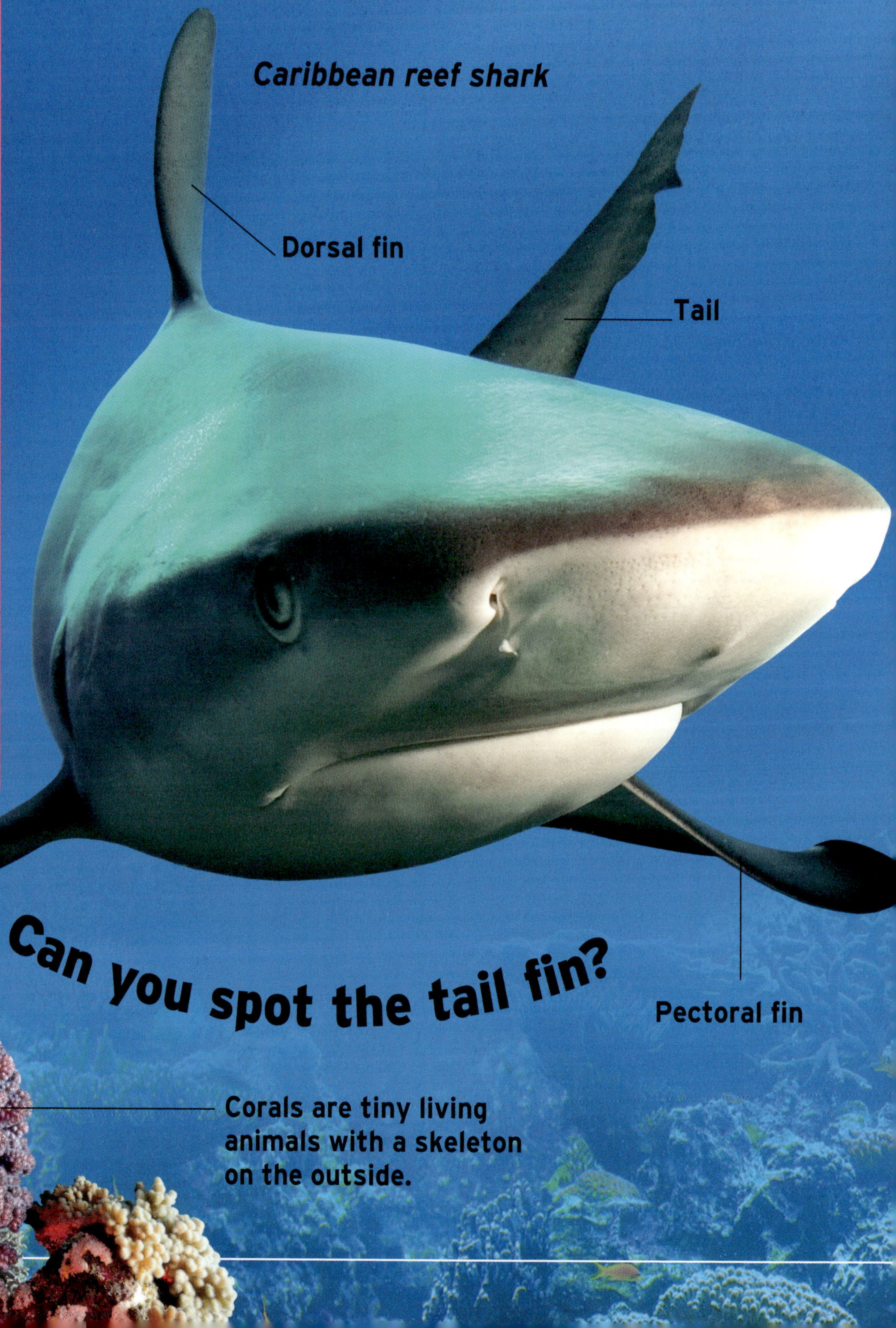

Fearsome friends

Blacktip reef sharks sometimes swim together on the reef to hunt their prey.

Blacktip reef sharks

Gray reef shark

These sharks are the fiercest predators on the reef. They are known for their ferocious feeding frenzies. They have even been known to eat each other!

Gray reef shark

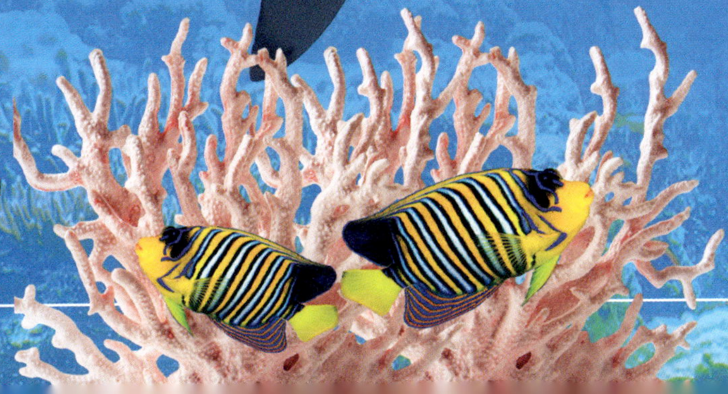

Two angelfish hide from a gray reef shark.

PREHISTORIC SHARK

One of the biggest and most powerful sharks that ever lived was called megalodon. Its name means "giant tooth." This shark is now extinct, but in prehistoric times it would have ruled the oceans. Megalodon's closest living relative is the great white.

What do you think it might have eaten?

Great white tooth

Megalodon tooth

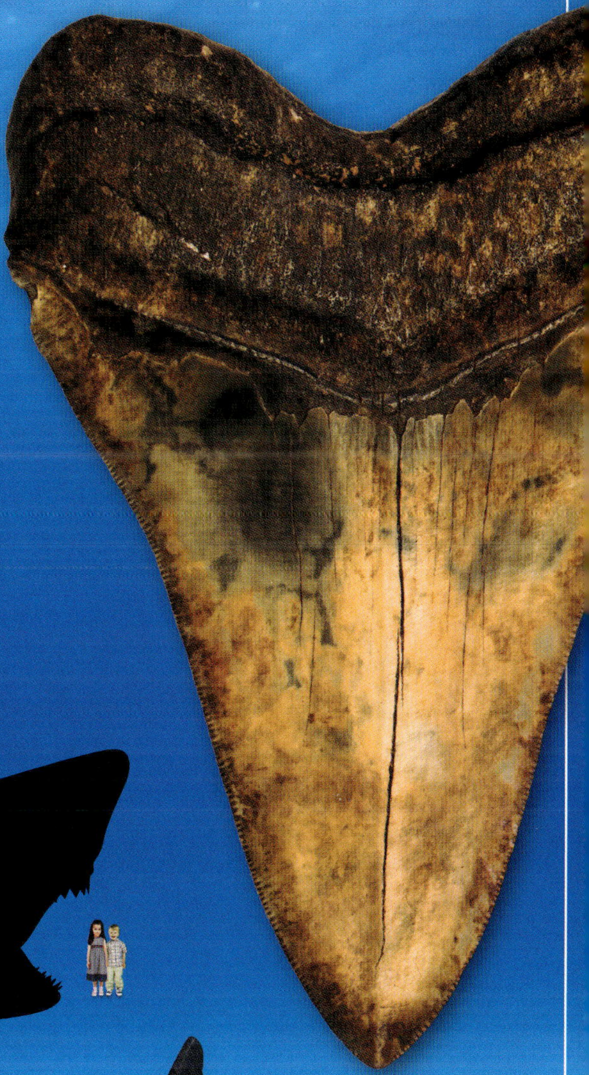

Biting power!

This is a fossil tooth belonging to megalodon. Look how big it is compared to the tooth of a great white! Thousands of megalodon teeth have been found all over the world.

Enormous size

Fossils suggest it might have reached 50 feet (15 m) long.

Big appetite

Megalodon would have preyed on prehistoric whales, dolphins, fish, and turtles.

SAVE OUR SHARKS!

The survival of many types of shark is now threatened by human activity, such as fishing and changes to their habitat (where they live). Some are caught by accident and some are hunted for their body parts, such as the jaws of great whites, which can be sold for high prices.

Great white shark

The numbers of whale sharks and scalloped hammerhead sharks are decreasing.

Fishing kills over 100 million sharks each year.

Extinction

Many young sharks are being killed before they have had a chance to have pups. This means some species may be threatened with extinction and could disappear from our oceans.

Shark soup

Many sharks are now in danger from people who catch them for sport or food—either for meat or to make shark fin soup.

Unhealthy sea

The sea is becoming an unhealthy place for sharks. The pollution of the oceans and the destruction of coral reefs damage the habitats that sharks need to live, feed, breed, and grow.

Once common in waters around Europe, the angel shark is now critically endangered.

What can we do?

Now that we know sharks are amazing animals, we need to do all we can to protect them!

GLOSSARY

Barbel – a fleshy "feeler" that grows from the mouth or snout of a fish.

Bioluminescence – the light produced by some living creatures, such as glowworms and deep-sea fish.

Camouflage – a pattern on an animal's skin that helps it to blend in with its surroundings.

Cartilage – a firm but flexible type of tissue in an animal's body. Human ears are made of cartilage.

Dorsal – positioned on the back or upper side of an animal.

Extinct – an animal or plant becomes extinct when all of its kind have died. Once that happens, the species is lost forever and cannot be brought back to life.

Pectoral – positioned on the chest area of an animal.

Plankton – tiny ocean animals and plants that make up the food for many larger animals.

Predator – an animal that hunts other animals.

Prehistoric – from a long, long time ago, before anything was written down.

Prey – an animal that is hunted by another animal.

Species – a group of animals or plants that are all of the same kind.

Index

angel shark 24–25, 30
barbels 8–9, 24
blacktip reef shark 5, 6, 27
blue shark 20–21
bull shark 14–15
camouflage 24–25
Caribbean reef shark 4, 26
coral reef 26–27, 31
denticles 5
diet 10–11, 17, 21, 23
dogfish 13
dorsal fin 6, 14–15, 26
dwarf lantern shark 4
extinction 28–29, 30–31
eyesight 8–9, 15
gray reef shark 27
great white shark 7, 9, 11, 15, 16–17, 28–29, 30
hammerhead shark 15, 18–19, 30
leopard shark 5, 25
megalodon 28–29
mermaid's purse 13
pectoral fin 6–7, 8, 24, 26
plankton 10
remora fish 23
teeth 11, 17, 22, 29
whale shark 4, 10, 22–23, 30